MANAGING WITHOUT
Weeds

MANAGING WITHOUT

Philip and Jean Talboys

SAWD
England

SAWD Publications
Placketts Hole, Bicknor,
Sittingbourne, Kent ME9 8BA.

ISBN: 1 872489 00 1

Printed in Great Britain
by Media Print, Sittingbourne, Kent.

CONTENTS

COLOUR ILLUSTRATIONS

Cover: Part of the author's garden, terraced with railway sleepers, and planted with herbaceous plants and ground cover for year-round interest.

INTRODUCTION

Coping with weeds is, all too often, the most laborious and time-consuming activity in the garden – never ending, like painting the Forth Bridge – and leaving little time for pleasant inactivity! But, with forethought and planning, and the application of a few simple principles and processes, the management of weeds can be reduced to a once-or-twice-a-year tidying-up operation.

This is not a book about how to kill weeds, but about how to manage a garden in such a way that weeds do not become a major problem. Although requiring initial cultivation, and a very limited and selective use of herbicides, the approach relies predominantly on methods that deprive weeds of the conditions they need if they are to flourish and compete successfully against our garden crop-plants and ornamentals. The aim is to prevent and avoid problems rather than to cure them.

A short account of the underlying principles of weed management is followed by chapters on cultivation, herbicides, mulches and – with particular emphasis – ground-cover plants. The final chapter 'Managing without weeds' brings together the various methods, and outlines a strategy for using them in combination to achieve a largely weed-free garden.

1 SOME BASIC FACTS AND PRINCIPLES

A weed has been conveniently defined as 'a plant growing where it is not wanted'! In this sense an oak seedling in a small urban garden is as much a weed as a poppy in a cornfield or ground elder in a herbaceous border. In practice, however, the weeds of most concern in day-to-day gardening are the all-prevailing annuals such as groundsel, bitter-cress, chickweed etc., and the pernicious perennials including nettles, thistles, dandelions, docks, couch-grass and ground elder.

The most characteristic feature of all common weeds is their capacity to occupy and exploit, very rapidly, any ground that is exposed and unprotected, and any other nook or cranny in which they can gain a foothold. They do this in two ways: by producing large numbers of seeds which can be dispersed near and far, and by vegetative growth, giving local spread immediately around an established plant, e.g. by creeping roots or creeping stems. Annual weeds spread almost exclusively by seed dispersal; perennials often exploit both options, although in some the production of seed is limited and vegetative spread predominates.

The capacity for seed production in weeds is illustrated by the following list which gives average numbers of seeds from a single well-developed plant:

groundsel	1,000	dandelion	5,000
chickweed	2,000	plantain	14,000
fat hen	3,000	dock	30,000
shepherd's purse	4,000	rosebay willowherb	80,000

Large plants obviously tend to produce more seeds than small ones, but some small plants have seeds that will germinate at any season, even in winter under mild conditions, and these will produce two or three generations in a year, with a total seed production greatly exceeding that of larger single-generation annuals. So, plants such as bitter cress, with its explosive seed capsules, and groundsel, with seeds bearing tufts of hairs that enable them to blow around in the wind, have a great capacity for spreading widely and occupying any available ground. Perennial weeds that are allowed to survive can produce a new crop of seed each year, and this greatly increases their ability to take advantage of any site that becomes available.

Obviously, the first principle for weed control is:

Do not allow weeds to get to the stage of producing and dispersing seeds.

If this precaution is neglected the number of seeds accumulating in the soil, to the depth of cultivation alone, can be more than 80,000 in every square metre.

Although some seeds, especially those of short-lived annual plants, germinate immediately they fall on the soil, many require a few weeks or months of dormancy before they will germinate. This helps to ensure that they survive the winter and germinate promptly in the spring, but seeds deeply buried in the soil have been known to remain dormant and survive for periods ranging for various plants from 2-3 years to more than 80 years, as the following examples show:

groundsel	2-3 years	chickweed	40 years
speedwell	5-10 years	plantain	40-50 years
shepherd's purse	30 years	poppy	80-100 years

Seeds stay dormant for as long as they remain either deeply buried or under other conditions that are unfavourable for germination, e.g. in heavily compacted soil. What makes a seed stay dormant is not fully understood, but the presence of too little oxygen and too much carbon dioxide seems to be important. These conditions can arise from the activity of the vast numbers of microscopic living organisms that occur in the soil, especially bacteria. However, as soon as soil is disturbed many of the dormant seeds germinate and develop into seedlings; digging or hoeing or any other form of cultivation therefore stimulates germination, and although hoeing destroys one batch of seedlings or established weeds it also ensures the development of a new flush of seedlings.

The effects of soil disturbance are seen most dramatically on major earthworks associated with motorway construction and other civil engineering projects, where embankments are often covered with poppies and orchids appear on motorway verges. The ploughing of a long-neglected pasture can also result in a spectacular flush of poppies where cereals had been grown long before the introduction of herbicides.

So, the second principle for weed control is:

Do not disturb the soil more than is absolutely necessary.

As well as considerations for seed production and dormancy, weed management in gardens has also to take into account the various other ways in which herbaceous perennial weeds and other 'unwanted' plants spread, multiply and 'overwinter'. The following are examples of vegetative structures that enable a plant to be an invasive weed.

Creeping roots:	perennial sow-thistle, creeping thistle, rosebay willowherb.
Creeping stems, above ground:	creeping buttercup, white clover lesser trefoil.
Creeping stems, underground:	yarrow, ground elder, stinging nettle, coltsfoot, couch-grass, yellow-flowered oxalis.
Bulbils*	pink-flowered oxalis.
Bulbs:	bluebell.
Tap-roots:	dandelion, dock.
Tubers, rhizomes and corms:	various persistent ornamental plants which may become 'unwanted'.

*Small and readily detachable buds, capable of developing into new plants.

All these structures can give rise to new plants when separated from the parent plant and may persist for a year, or more, if buried in the soil. Extensive systems of creeping roots and stems are often brittle and readily broken up into small fragments when the soil is cultivated, each piece being capable of becoming an independent new plant. Any part of a dandelion tap-root can form a new plant, but only the upper parts of those of dock.

It is worth bearing in mind that the features of a plant that make it an invasive weed are the same as those that in other circumstances make an effective and desirable ground-cover plant *(see Chapter 6)*. Indeed some plants such as the pink-flowered oxalis and ground elder (particularly a variegated form) can be regarded as pernicious weeds or desirable ground-covers, according to taste!

Deeply buried root and stem fragments tend to remain in a dormant state, like seeds, although for less extended periods, and are stimulated into growth when the soil is disturbed. Therefore, although hoeing and digging destroy all the parts of perennial weeds that are removed and burnt, these cultivations can also assist their multiplication and spread and encourage the growth of plant fragments that have been lying dormant in the soil. This is why it is much more difficult to eradicate perennial weeds than annuals.

Therefore, the next principle for weed control is:

Give top priority to eliminating perennial weeds.

Methods of dealing with them effectively are discussed later *(see Chapter 4)*.

Even the best kept garden is vunerable to the accidental introduction of weeds from outside. Obviously there is nothing that can be done to prevent air-borne seeds from blowing in over the fence. Weeds creeping in **under** the fence may have to be attacked chemically *(see Chapter 4)*. But it is all too easy to introduce pernicious weeds with plants bought from a nursery or garden centre, or brought in from the gardens of friends and neighbours. One particularly 'vicious' weed the yellow-flowered oxalis *(Oxalis corniculatus)* is sold in some garden centres as an ornamental plant, and is a rather frequent weed in others. It has explosive seed capsules that propel the seed for a metre or more, so any potted plants in their vicinity may well be carrying seeds of this weed even if seedlings are not already visible. It is worth taking care not to introduce this weed if it is not already present in the garden. Other 'unwelcome guests' in the garden include microscopic insects and fungi etc that can be introduced on plant roots or in soil. Although not usually visible to the naked eye their effects on the plant may be obvious, and any plant showing abnormal yellowing or death of leaves or rotting of the stem base or roots is better not accepted, even as a gift!

2 GERMINATION, DEVELOPMENT AND ESTABLISHMENT OF WEEDS

A plant developing below the soil surface, whether from a seed or some vegetative part, will generally have access to most of its main growth requirements, i.e. water, mineral elements, oxygen and carbon dioxide, but it can only utilise these to become established and to develop into a mature plant if it can gain access to light. By the process of photosynthesis the plant is able to convert light energy into the chemical energy required for all the other living processes, by means of which an acorn becomes an oak tree, and a weed seed becomes a weed. During the period between the germination of a seed and the emergence of the seedling above the soil surface into the light, all energy needs are met from the reserves of starch etc. stored in the seed. Similarly a perennial developing from a buried vegetative part (rhizome, bulbil, etc.) relies on the energy sources stored in it, until it reaches the light.

So the fourth principle for weed control is:

Do not let the weeds 'see' the sky.

Most weed seeds are small, or very small, and their reserves are therefore only enough for a very brief period of development between germination and emergence into the light. This means that they can only emerge through a very shallow layer of soil; if they germinate deeper they will die before reaching the light. Larger seeds will emerge from greater depths, but the majority of seeds develop from within the upper 20mm of the soil, and few from a depth of more than 50mm. Some plants even require light for germination and will only germinate on the soil surface.

Energy reserves in the overwintering parts of herbaceous perennial plants are generally much greater than those of seeds, and consequently the shoots are able to emerge from greater depths in the soil, provided that conditions are otherwise satisfactory, and in particular that oxygen is readily available, circumstances that are likely to result especially from digging and other forms of cultivation. Weed 'management' is aimed at ensuring that conditions for growth and establishment remain as

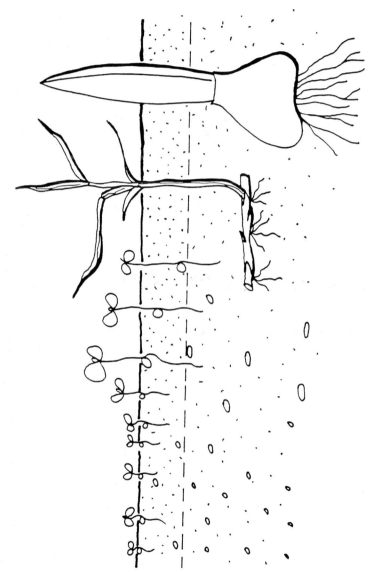

Fig 1. Most weed seeds germinate only at or near the soil surface. Established perennial weeds, and other plants with substantial underground food reserves, can emerge from greater depths.

PLATE ONE:

Top: *Acaena microphylla*   p.36

Middle: *Ajuga reptans*   p.36

Bottom: *Asarum europaeum*   p.37

PLATE TWO:

Top: *Campanula poscharskyana* p.38

Middle: *Cotoneaster dammeri* p.3?

Bottom: *Cotula squalida* p.39

unsuitable as possible. The difficulty is that the conditions favouring the growth of weeds are generally the same as those required for the growth of the vegetables, flowers, trees and shrubs that are *wanted* in the garden.

However, the facts about plant growth and development that have been discussed above with particular reference to weeds, i.e. seed production and dispersal, seed dormancy and longevity, vegetative growth and the means of survival of perennials in winter or other unfavourable conditions, and the requirements for germination, development and emergence into light, can be exploited in methods of garden management aimed at minimizing the effort of controlling weeds.

Several different approaches to weed control will be dealt with in the following chapters on cultivation, herbicides, mulches and ground-cover plants; and in the final chapter, various combinations of these methods will be discussed, with the aim of minimizing both labour and the use of chemicals.

3 CULTIVATION FOR WEED CONTROL

Cultivation, bringing about the physical destruction of weeds, is the traditional method of weed control; at the same time it breaks up the soil surface to varying depths, depending on whether hand pulling, hoeing, or digging with a fork or spade is used to deal with deep-rooted perennials, or one of the wide range of other hand- or machine-operated aids to cultivation now available in garden centres. In addition to weed control, cultivation enables a fine tilth to be established, giving the neat and tidy appearance much appreciated by many keen gardeners, and providing good seed-bed conditions. However, the effectiveness of weed control depends on the timing and frequency of the operations. Ideally, hoeing should be carried out when the weeds are at the seedling stage, and in any case before they have flowered and produced new seeds. *Cultivation after flowering will ensure maximum dispersal of seeds* and burial in the soil. Attack at an early stage will also help to ensure that seedlings of perennial weeds are destroyed before they have produced tap-roots or creeping stems or roots that will help them to persist or survive in the soil.

It is vital to remember that, as well as destroying existing weed seedlings, every cultivation stimulates the germination of dormant seeds and encourages the development of buried fragments of perennial weeds. It is therefore essential to *cultivate regularly and frequently* if efficient weed control is to be achieved by this method alone.

There is an old saying:

"one year's seeding means seven years' weeding"

There is a considerable element of truth in this statement. Provided that seeding is prevented by regular cultivation there is a progressive reduction in the number of seeds remaining in the soil at the normal depth of cultivation. But if management is neglected the number of seeds can rise to perhaps 80,000–100,000 over every square metre. Research on a wide range of weed species has shown that *on average*, the number of seeds present in the soil within the depth of cultivation is reduced

11

by about 50% each year under regular and frequent cultivation. If we consider a small area of soil containing 100 seeds initially, the number will fall in successive years approximately thus:

	100→	50→	25→	12→	6→	3→	2→	1	
after	0	1	2	3	4	5	6	7	years

so that, in theory, the number should be negligible after 7 years. However, there will inevitably be some 'fall-out' of seeds carried by the wind and other agencies, and fragments of perennial weeds broken up and dispersed by the cultivations themselves, may well persist indefinitely. Clearly, one year's neglect can undo the benefits of many years' diligent work.

Weed control by cultivation can be an effective and rewarding occupation for gardeners with time and the inclination to make it a frequent and regular routine and also provides the great pleasure of the sight of a neatly 'manicured' garden. It is particularly appropriate in vegetable gardens, where the straight lines and even spacing can be adapted conveniently to the dimensions of the available tools. But for many people the time and labour involved is not an acceptable option: For them, all is not lost! The rest of the book is dedicated to them!

4 HERBICIDES

To many people weedkillers are '*A Bad Thing*'! Used indiscriminately this may be true, but with limited, selective and careful use, in line with the instructions on the bottle or packet, they can be a valuable aid to garden management without any adverse effects.

It is better to use the term 'herbicide' rather than 'weedkiller', as a reminder that the chemicals do not just kill weeds. It is also important to remember that they do not all do the same job, that they work in different ways, and that it is necessary to select the most appropriate type for the task in hand. From the practical point of view the most important differences are between *contact herbicides* and *systemic herbicides*, both of which are applied to the plants, and *residual herbicides* which are applied to the soil.

The best-known *contact herbicide* is a paraquat/diquat mixture. When sprayed on a plant it kills any green tissue with which it comes in contact, leaves and young stems rapidly turning bright yellow before collapsing and rotting. It has no effect on woody stems of trees and shrubs and does not kill the roots. Herbicides of this type are very effective against annual weeds, because the roots of annuals do not survive if the top is killed, and they can be used with care amongst established herbaceous plants and shrubs, on which a few accidentally spotted leaves have no long-term damaging effect. Contact herbicides can also be used between rows of vegetables, given suitable methods of application: these will be discussed later.

Sprays of *systemic herbicides* penetrate into leaves and young stems and then move within the plant to parts that have not received any spray, including the roots. They are slower-acting than the contact herbicides, but they eventually kill both the top and the roots of treated plants. They are therefore effective against perennial plants as well as annuals. They may be *selective*, like the hormone weed-killer 2,4-D which can be used to kill broad-leaved weeds in lawns without damaging the grass, and alloxydim-sodium which will eliminate couch-grass amongst herbaceous plants and shrubs. Other systemic herbicides are *non-*

selective; glyphosate is of this type, and it will kill a very wide range of both broad-leaved plants and grasses. This is a most useful substance and might well be called *'the gardener's friend'*, although *if carelessly applied* it can kill herbaceous ornamentals, shrubs and sometimes even trees. It has no residual effect in the soil.

Residual herbicides are normally applied to a weed-free soil surface, after either cultivation or treatment with contact or systemic herbicides to eliminate existing weeds. The residual chemical then kills seedlings as they germinate. An application, e.g. of simazine or dichlobenil, early in the year will keep the ground free from most weeds throughout the growing season. Although they can be used to supress weeds under roses, shrubs etc., the soil surface must then remain bare and undisturbed throughout the season. In 'minimal chemistry' gardening the residual herbicides are of limited application, but they can usefully be used to maintain weed-free paths and a weed-free strip along the base of a fence.

Detailed information on the use of herbicides as the main method of weed control in gardens is available in the publications listed at the end of this chapter, but for the purpose of this book the main use of herbicides is for the control of perennial weeds.

Perennial weeds in cultivated ground

Because of their capacity to persist in the soil in a vegetative state, with substantial energy reserves and therefore an ability to emerge from a greater depth than most seedlings, perennial weeds can present a recurring problem in a 'weed management' garden unless they are eliminated as the first priority. This can be achieved most easily in areas that do not contain any plants that need to be retained, using the following schedule:

(1) Spray all the plants in the plot with glyphosate, ideally starting early in the season when weed growth is vigorous. It will take 2-3 weeks for most plants to show severe signs of damage, but by this time the chemical will be well distributed within the plants. When they are obviously dying the plot can be dug or thoroughly cultivated and the plant-remains removed and burnt.

Soon a new flush of weeds will appear, many of them seedlings but also some perennials, arising from surviving fragments of those treated earlier and some from pieces that have lain dormant deeper in the soil.

(2) 6-8 weeks after the initial treatment, depending on the rate of growth of new weeds, spray again with glyphosate, wait 2-3 weeks, then cultivate again.

(3) 6-8 weeks after the second treatment spray with glyphosate for the third time, but refrain from further cultivation: merely remove any unsightly dead weeds with minimal disturbance.

These operations will largely eradicate perennial weeds, including couch-grass, but a few more resistant weeds may continue to appear and will require spot-treatment either with glyphosate or with one of the hormone weed-killers, e.g. 2,4-D. Remember, however, that these hormone preparations may leave a residue in the soil for a few weeks which could damage sensitive plants. Glyphosate leaves no residues in the soil.

Having eliminated most perennial weeds – and, incidently, many annuals – it is necessary to take steps to prevent, as far as is possible, their re-establishment. The options include cultivation *(see page 11)*, continued use of herbicides, weed-free mulches *(see page 21)* or ground-cover plants *(see page 27)*.

Similar methods to eliminate perennial weeds can be adopted, with care, under shrubs or around trees, provided that glyphosate is not allowed to make contact with leaves or unhardened stems of the trees and shrubs. Amongst herbaceous plants the method is more difficult to apply. Spot-treatment of isolated perennial weeds may require the use of a screened spray-jet *(see page 19)* to protect plants that are to be retained: alternatively a gel-formulation of glyphosate can be painted on the leaves of weeds, making sure that none is transferred to valuable plants, e.g. by treated weeds being blown in contact with them before the 'paint' is dry, or by accidental 'drips' from the paint-brush.

A more radical solution in a weed-infested herbaceous bed or border is to take out the plants that are needed and to proceed with a full 'cleaning-up' operation with glyphosate, as described above; meanwhile propagate selected material in a weed-free compost for eventual replanting. It is best to propagate the plants from small pieces that appear to be free from any creeping roots or stems of weeds or, better still when possible, to use only cuttings taken from above ground level, to avoid transferring weed seeds from the soil. Using such precautions the risk of re-introducing perennial weeds to a treated bed should be minimal. Replanting with plants from a nursery or garden centre requires careful selection of well-managed material *(see pages 4-5)*.

Where couch-grass is the main problem in herbaceous borders, shrubberies etc. a **selective** chemical, alloxydim-sodium, can be sprayed overall to kill the grass without damaging valuable broad-leaved plants.

Perennial weeds in lawns and rough grass

Selective chemicals are generally required for controlling perennial weeds in lawns, although isolated dandelions or plantains can be painted with the gel preparation of glyphosate. Sprays or granules based on a mixture of 2,4-D with dicamba, dichlorprop, mecoprop or fenoprop are usually effective, when applied strictly as described in the instructions on the bottle or packet. These materials are most effective when the grass and weeds are growing rapidly, hence the practice of combining herbicides with fertilizers for lawn treatments. There may, however, be some advantage in separate applications, with the fertilizer first so that its effects are well developed before the herbicide is put on; fewer treatments may then be needed.

Coarse perennial weeds (nettles, docks, thistles) in orchard grass, paddocks etc. can be treated with mixtures of selective weedkillers based on 2,4-D. For large areas of rough grass there may be a case for using one of the very effective mixtures of herbicides available for use in agriculture but, legally, these can only be applied by a person who has a Certificate of Competence in the Use of Pesticides, issued by the National Proficiency Tests Council for Agriculture and Horticulture.

PLATE THREE:

Top: *Erica* cultivars and *Juniperus squamata* 'Blue Star' (with *Chamaecyparis lawsoniana* 'Forsteckensis') p.40, p46

Middle: *Euphorbia amygdaloides robbiae* p.40

Bottom: *Gaultheria procumbens* p.41

PLATE FOUR:

Top: *Geranium sanguineum* p.42

Middle: *Hacquetia epipactis* p.42

Bottom: *Hebe pinguifolia*
'Pagei' p.43

An agricultural supplier may be able to recommend a suitably qualified contractor to do the job. Note also that domestic grass-eating animals (horses, donkeys, goats, etc) should be kept off herbicide-treated pasture because poisonous plants such as ragwort become much more palatable when they are dying after herbicide treatment, and are more likely to be eaten than when they are growing normally.

Total weed control for non-planted sites

Management of footpaths, gravel drives, the ground under fences and sometimes under hedges may require the complete exclusion of all plants. For this purpose the residual herbicides giving nearly year-long suppression of plant growth can be useful. They are normally applied after the ground has been cleared of weeds, either by cultivation or by the use of contact or systemic herbicides, but a number of commercial preparations for 'total' control contain either paraquat/diquat (contact herbicide) or amino-triazine (systemic) together with the long-term residual herbicide, simazine. Simazine can also be used alone, after cultivation or, for example, after treatment with glyphosate, which has advantages because simazine does not give complete control of established perennial weeds, even at the high dose-rates applicable for treatment of paths. Simazine preparations are normally applied as suspensions in water, although there is now a granular form which is simply scattered on the soil surface. Another granular material, easy to apply and very effective for year-long total control, is dichlobenil. It suppresses annual and most perennial weeds.

At lower dose rates both simazine and dichlobenil can be used for weed control under roses, many shrubs (but not all) and under some hedges, but they cannot be used if bulbs or ground-cover plants are being grown, nor if the shrubs are to be mulched. Once treated with a residual herbicide the soil surface must be left undisturbed throughout the season, both to maintain herbicide action and to prevent the chemical coming into contact with the roots of the shrubs and causing damage. Waterlogging of treated soil can also result in herbicide damage to the shrubs.

Methods of applying herbicides

The first essential for safe handling of herbicides (and any other garden chemicals) is to follow precisely the instructions provided on the container. In particular it is important to use the correct dose-rates and not to 'add a little bit extra to make sure'! **Too much** of a herbicide can make it **less effective**, especially with systemics; if the leaves are killed too quickly the chemical may not move sufficiently to affect the whole plant, especially the roots, and defeats the object of using a systemic herbicide. However a higher rate **may** be needed (as shown in the instructions) for any weeds which are not eliminated at the lower dose-rate.

The other important aspect is the method of applying herbicides, so that only the 'target' plants are treated and killed. This needs precise 'placement' and minimum 'drift', together with a minimum of wasteful run-off into the soil. These are all determined by the size of the droplets produced by the sprayer or by the rose or dribble-bar on a watering-can. Small drops give good coverage of the foliage and little run-off, but can drift readily in the wind. Large drops do not drift appreciably but tend to give a drenching effect with considerable run-off, and use large amounts of the diluted spray material. For this reason the rate of dilution of the herbicide with water for spray-application is different from that for watering-can use.*

When a herbicide needs to be used on weeds close to vunerable vegetable crops or amongst herbaceous flowering plants, there is less risk of accident with the large drops from a dribble-bar on a watering-can than from the use of a sprayer, especially in unexpected gusts of wind. However, for many purposes it is more convenient to use a pressurised sprayer, with a jet that can be adjusted to give a moderate or coarse spray to reduce the risk of drift. It is **always** undesirable to spray under windy conditions, but even a light breeze can carry a very fine spray a considerable distance.

*E.g. glyphosate (applied as Tumbleweed) is used at 90ml in 1 litre for use in a sprayer, and at 90ml in 4 litres for watering-can application; each is sufficient to treat approximately 30sq. metres of weed-covered ground.

Spot treatment of isolated weeds, e.g. in a herbaceous border, can be done safely with a sprayer if a conical or pyramidal hood is attached to the spray jet to confine the spray. Some commercial spray-kits include a detachable hood, but otherwise a satisfactory screen can be constructed from a plastic funnel with the stem shortened and attached to the spray jet. When using such an attachment it is necessary to give only a short burst of spray, otherwise an excessive amount runs down the sides of the screen on to the ground. Care is also needed to ensure that when the sprayer is moved, no drips of herbicide run off the edge of the hood on to valuable plants in the vicinity; it should be kept near the ground while in use.

Two other points are worth noting: Firstly, it is very desirable to keep a separate watering-can or sprayer to use **only** for herbicides; otherwise very thorough washing of equipment with a household detergent and large amounts of water is **essential**, and should be done immediately after use.

Secondly, when using a fine rose or a dribble-bar on a watering-can, make sure that it is firmly attached, and try it out with water, before using the herbicide. The action, particularly with a full watering-can, is sometimes unexpectedly sudden, and if the dribble-bar is incorrectly adjusted, the herbicide may land in quite the wrong place with the possibility of disastrous consequences!

Other ways of applying glyphosate to individual weed plants include wearing a rubber glove, wetting it with diluted herbicide or the gel-preparation, and then stroking the weed gently with the gloved hand. A commercial 'spot applicator' comprising a reservoir of herbicide leading to an absorbent pad is also available for spot treatment of weeds.

Residual herbicides persist on and near the soil surface for long periods because they dissolve only very slowly. Therefore, if they are to be applied in water they cannot be dissolved but are made into a milky suspension of very fine solid particles. These particles tend to block a sprayer, so a watering-can with a fine rose or dribble-bar must be used. The suspension should be kept well-mixed and used rapidly once it is made-up, otherwise it may tend to block even the relatively coarse holes in the dribble-bar and this can result in uneven application.

Granular preparations are easier to apply, with either a wheeled applicator, as used for lawn fertilizers and weed-killers, or from a 'pepper-pot' dispenser, which can be home-made by drilling several suitable sized holes in the plastic lid of a screw-top container. It is essential to use a container with a firmly attached lid to ensure that a large mass of herbicide is not accidently deposited on the ground. Care is needed to apply the correct amount of chemical, especially if it is to be used amongst shrubs etc. The area to be treated should be marked off in square metres (or yards), and the required amount weighed into a small scoop or measure that can then be marked to indicate the **volume** required per square metre (or yard), instead of repeated weighings. Although with practice it may be thought possible to judge the corrrect dose 'by eye' this is an unreliable method and cannot be recommended, especially where there are valuable plants.

The place of herbicides in 'minimal chemistry' weed management.

Although herbicides can be used for all weed control requirements in the garden, and with careful use will not have long-term adverse effects, many people will prefer to use alternative methods requiring little or no herbicide, i.e. cultivation, mulches, or ground-cover plants. However, any of these methods of management can benefit from the specific uses of herbicides outlined above: a non-persistent systemic herbicide (e.g. glyphosate) to eliminate perennial weeds as the starting-point for the other methods; and a persistent residual herbicide (eg simazine or dichlobenil) to keep paths and other non-planted areas free from vegetation throughout the year.

ADDITIONAL INFORMATION

Weed Control in the Garden, by R. Chancellor. A Wisley Handbook (Cassell).
Plant Protection in the Garden, Edited by G.W. Ivens, J. Stubbs & Scientific Staff, R.H.S. Wisley. (British Crop Protection Council and R.H.S.) (Publication: Spring 1990).

5   MULCHES

Mulching has long been used as a method of conserving soil moisture. Traditional advice has been to spread a 3-inch layer of half-rotted farmyard manure, well-rotted vegetable refuse, leaf-mould, grass mowings, coconut fibre, spent hops etc. over soil around growing plants. Today the list would also include peat, composted bark, wood chippings, grit, pebbles and black polythene sheeting, and the emphasis now is as much on weed control as on water-conservation.

The main effect of mulches in weed control is to exclude light from weed seedlings. We have already seen that most weed seeds germinate and emerge into the light from the top few centimetres of the soil, and that they have insufficient food reserves to emerge from greater depths. If a layer of compost is placed over the soil surface to a depth of several centimetres, then even the seedlings germinating near the soil surface will mostly fail to reach the light and will die. Those buried more deeply will remain dormant, no further cultivation will be needed, and no more seeds will be stimulated to germinate. But a mulch will only provide a weed-free surface if it is itself free from weeds. Farmyard manure and the products of the garden compost-heap frequently contain numerous viable weed seeds and are therefore unsuitable as a weed-controlling mulch, even though they conserve moisture. Spent hops, spent mushroom compost, peat, composted bark, wood chippings, grit and pebbles generally contain few weed seeds and are therefore suitable for suppressing annual weeds. Whatever mulch is used, it is necessary to 'top-up' with extra material at least once a year, particularly so with organic materials which become broken down and incorporated in the soil by the action of fungi, bacteria, insects, earthworms etc. However this process is relatively slow when wood chippings or composted bark are used.

Like other methods of controlling weeds, mulches do not suppress perennial plants that persist in the soil as more or less massive vegetative structures with substantial food reserves. Therefore, as with other methods, it is essential to eliminate perennial weeds before applying the mulch. Here also the use of a systemic herbicide such as glyphosate is the most satisfatory method of destroying unwanted perennial weeds

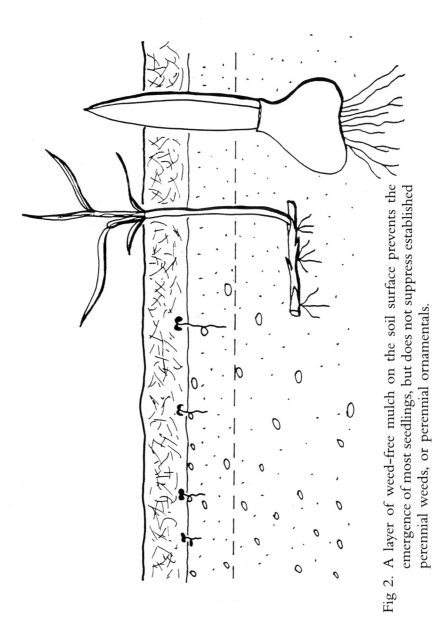

Fig 2. A layer of weed-free mulch on the soil surface prevents the emergence of most seedlings, but does not suppress established perennial weeds, or perennial ornamentals.

and other plants. Nevertheless, the ability of perennial plants to penetrate a mulch makes it practicable to manage bulbs, herbaceous borders etc. by this method, with minimal labour.

Sheets of black polythene will suppress weeds in the same way as other mulches, as long as they remain intact, but in ornamental gardens they are generally considered unsightly. There has to be some means of holding them in place, either by burying the edges (which then become weedy) or placing stones or bricks etc. at intervals. Black polythene can usefully be used for spaced plants in vegetable and fruit growing, most effectively by placing the sheets in position before planting, then making slits through which the plants can be inserted into the soil; but note that walking over black polythene on stony ground can cause numerous perforations. Once well established, strawberries etc will hold the plastic mulch in place. Water retention under polythene is generally excellent, but on light soils it may be desirable to incorporate trickle irrigation lines under the polythene. However, new sheet materials have recently become available which suppress weed development but are permeable to water, and therefore allow the passage of rain or sprinkler-applied water into the soil.

One important word of caution: Never apply a mulch of any kind around trees or shrubs where a residual herbicide (simazine, dichlobenil etc.) has been used within the previous year or two. Plant roots tend to spread upwards towards a mulch and can therefore come into contact with any residual herbicide on the soil surface: this can sometimes result in severe damage to the plant.

Mulches can often usefully be used as a temporary measure to control weeds in newly planted areas where ground-cover plants, herbaceous borders etc. are being established and have not yet developed a complete canopy to exclude the light from the soil surface. A mulch of grit or pebbles is especially beneficial for many alpine plants because it both conserves moisture in the root-zone and maintains relatively dry conditions around the crown of the plant, where rotting is frequently a major problem if conditions are excessively wet in winter. It is often not appreciated that in their natural habitat many alpine plants spend at least an 8-month 'winter' under a layer of snow at a temperature a few degrees below freezing. Under these conditions they are effectively

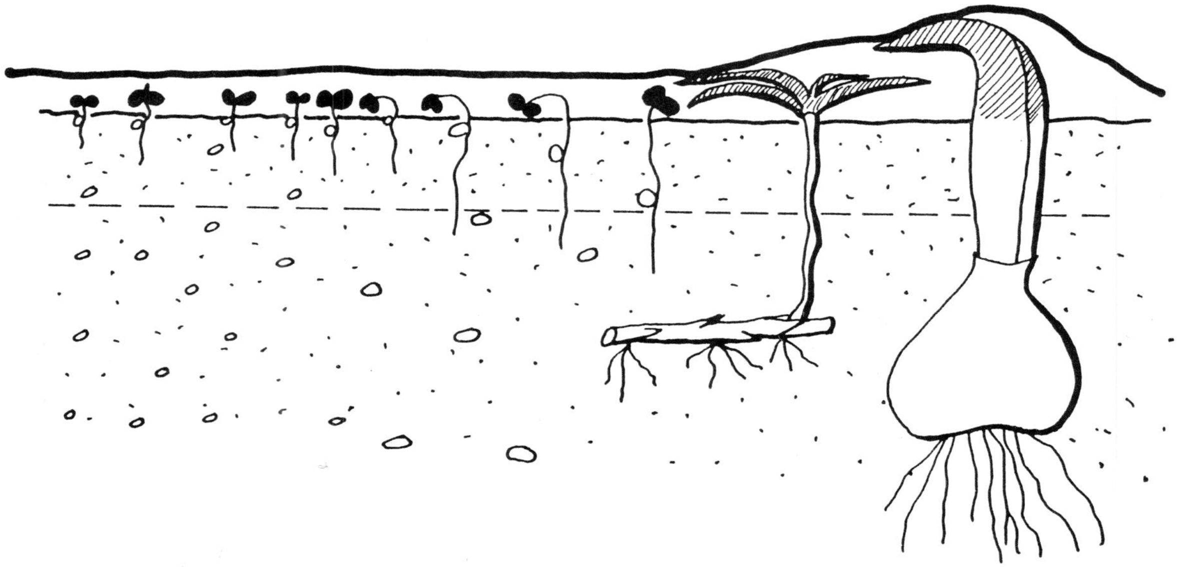

Fig 3. A sheet of black polythene placed over the soil surface will suppress seedling emergence and also the development of perennial plants.

24

'dry', but do not 'dry out', or desiccate because the protective layer of snow prevents evaporation. As well as suppressing competitive weeds, a thick mulch of grit or pebbles goes some way towards helping alpines survive the wet conditions and fluctuating temperatures of lowland winters, paradoxically more 'difficult' than high alpine conditions.

Although the action of mulches in preventing the growth of weeds from seeds already present in the soil is mainly through the exclusion of light, this clearly does not account for any suppression of seeds blown in from the neighbourhood. The fact that such 'invasions' do not generally seem to be a major problem suggests that the surface layers of most weed-free mulching materials are fairly unfavourable for seed germination and seedling establishment, probably because they tend to dry out rapidly and have little readily-available nutrient content. A seed germinating on the surface has plenty of light, but its root must penetrate to the soil before it can obtain the mineral nutrients that it also needs for vigorous growth. The mulch thus acts a barrier in both directions. The few weeds that succeed in becoming established can usually be removed from a mulch with little disturbance. Nutrient-rich organic mulches such as farmyard manure and garden compost are more likely than peat, spent mushroom compost, composted bark, wood chippings, grit etc., to be colonised by wind-borne weeds as well as by the weed seeds carried within the mulch.

6   GROUND-COVER PLANTS

However effective the weed-suppressing properties of mulches may be, their appearance has only a limited appeal for most plant-lovers. Ground-cover plants enable essentially the same principles to be exploited, but provide a great diversity of colour and form, without the need for frequent 'topping-up' or replacement.

An effective ground-cover plant needs to be a hardy, rapidly-spreading perennial, preferably evergreen, giving dense and complete cover of the ground in 1 - 2 years. Its effect resembles that of a mulch in that it excludes light from any seedlings that may germinate on or near the soil surface. Also, many ground-cover plants have dense root systems colonising the surface layers of the soil and competing strongly for water and nutrients as well as for light. Such competition may account for the fact that even thinly 'encrusting' ground-cover plants such as *Raoulia* species *(see page 49)* can be remarkably effective in suppressing weeds. As with a good mulch, and provided that perennial weeds have been eliminated, a well-developed ground-cover removes the necessity for cultivation, with its accompanying stimulation of weed seed germination, while permitting the development of ornamental perennials from bulbs, corms, tubers and rhizomes etc. In addition to suppressing weeds, many ground-cover plants are valuable in preventing soil erosion, especially on sloping ground. An interwoven carpet of roots or stems binds the soil, impedes the flow of surface water in heavy rain, and protects the soil surface from being disturbed by the impact of rain drops.

The expression 'ground-cover plant' is sometimes used only to describe low-growing perennials that form a 'carpet' over the soil surface. However, in relation to weed control it seems reasonable to use it for any plant that grows sufficiently densely to prevent light from falling directly on the soil surface throughout most of the growing season; it is used in this broad sense throughout this book, excluding only annual plants, which depend on re-seeding for any long-term effect.

Types of ground-cover plants

The effectiveness of ground-cover plants for suppressing weeds (and for preventing erosion) depends on their rate of spread and density of cover; these in turn depend on the type of growth – herbaceous or

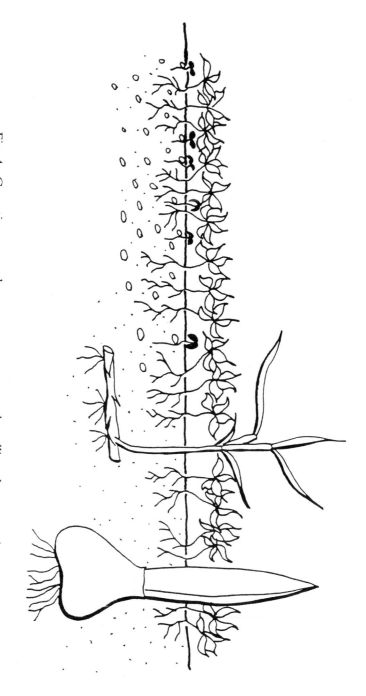

Fig 4. Carpeting ground-cover suppresses weed seedlings by competing for light, water and nutrients, but established perennial weeds, and ornamental plants, can grow through the cover.

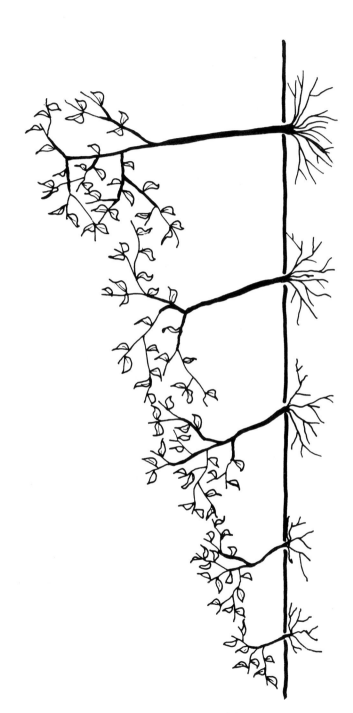

Fig 5. Plants that form a sufficiently dense canopy to exclude much of the light from the soil surface, even if they are not 'conventional' ground-cover plants, will effectively suppress all but the most vigorous weeds.

shrubby, evergreen or deciduous – and the ways in which they spread over the ground. Several main types can be recognised:-

(1) **Prostrate, non-rooting ground-cover:** Evergreen or deciduous shrubs with one or a few main stems giving rise (a) to a dense growth of predominantly prostrate branches, or (b) to a more or less hemispherical 'hummock' of which the lowest branches are prostrate; mostly they do not root down on contact with the soil, and sometimes are relatively slow-growing. The group also includes shrubby plants that form a many-stemmed hummock, (c) of which only the outer shoots are more or less prostrate. Examples include prostrate or dwarf conifers, heathers, some cotoneasters, *Lonicera pileata*, etc.

(2) **Prostrate, rooting ground-cover:** Prostrate evergreen or deciduous plants, branching to form a dense cover and developing roots at many or most stem nodes ('joints') in contact with the soil or leaf litter, but having no specialised 'creeping' parts; they have a moderate or rapid rate of spread. The plants may form short, erect flower-bearing shoots, or flower directly on the prostrate shoots. eg. prostrate willows, dwarf periwinkles, thymes, etc.

(3) **Creeping, herbaceous or shrubby ground-cover:** Evergreen or deciduous plants, spreading by means of creeping roots, or by surface-growing or subterranean creeping stems that form roots at many or most 'joints', and give rise to erect flower-bearing shoots either directly or after forming leafy rosettes on the soil surface. These specialised 'colonisers' spread rapidly, sometimes becoming invasive. eg. lamiums, bugles, etc. Some perennial weeds have all these characteristics and can form effective 'ground-cover' eg. ground elder *(Aegopodium podagraria)*, a species that is used for this purpose – especially the variegated form – in N. America.

(4) **Herbaceous clump-forming ground-cover:** Herbaceous perennial plants forming gradually-expanding clumps or 'crowns', rapidly producing dense leaf-cover and flower-bearing shoots in spring and summer, but dying down in winter. eg. alchemillas, day-lilies, hellebores, hostas, etc.

(5) **Trailing, thicket-forming ground-cover:** Deciduous or evergreen plants with trailing stems, often only sparsley branched and

rooting down infrequently, eventually forming an extensive thicket unless curtailed. but often slow to control weeds effectively. eg. roses, *Rubus* spp., etc.

Groups (2) and (3) include most of the so-called 'carpeting' and 'colonising' ground-cover plants.

Establishment of ground-cover plants

Ideally, ground-cover plants should provide a complete cover within one or two years of planting. Meanwhile other measures will be required to control weeds in the spaces between them. The time taken to achieve complete cover depends on the rate at which the plants grow and the planting distance between them. Obviously a slow-growing plant needs much closer spacing than a fast-growing one, and therefore it takes many more plants to cover the required area; this can be expensive. The aim can be achieved with maximum economy and minimal frustration by buying a few well-grown plants from groups (2) and (3), dividing them into small portions which are then grown on in pots or trays before planting out. During the time required for these divisions to develop good root systems, the chosen planting site can be cleared of perennial weeds completely. This is **essential** for minimal maintenance management thereafter. Plants from group (1) usually need to be propagated by cuttings which may take at least two years to reach planting size. Those in group (4) can be increased by planting out in nursery beds for a growing season to develop into clumps that can be divided into a number of pieces before planting out in their permanent site. The schedule outlined on pages 14-15 for using a systemic herbicide such as glyphosate to clean-up before mulching is also applicable in preparation for planting ground-cover. Effort expended at this stage is a 'capital investment' that pays valuable 'dividends' for years ahead!

There is considerable advantage in planting out the ground-cover at the same time as other plants on the cleaned-up site, whether trees, shrubs, herbaceous plants etc., and any bulbs that are to emerge through the ground-cover. Simultaneous planting avoids the necessity for digging holes for planting at a later stage, with the possibility of stimulating further weed growth around the newly planted material. The stimulation

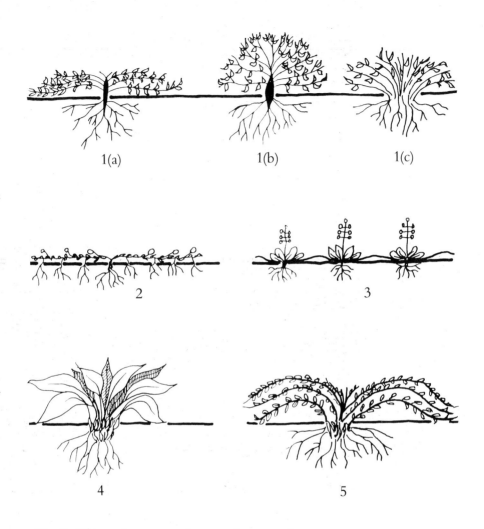

Fig 6. The main types of ground-cover plants:
   (1) *Prostrate, mostly non-rooting.* (a) typical prostrate form; (b) hummock-forming, from one or a few shoots, only the lowest shoots prostrate; (c) multi-stemmed hummock, only the outer shoots prostrate.
   (2) *Prostrate, rooting-down.*
   (3) *Creeping, herbaceous or shrubby.*
   (4) *Herbaceous, clump-forming.*
   (5) *Trailing, thicket-forming.*

PLATE FIVE:

Top: *Hosta fortunei* (with *Helleborus orientalis*) p.44

Middle: *Houttuynia cordata* 'Flore Pleno' p.44

Bottom: *Pachysandra terminalis* p.47

PLATE SIX:

Top: *Phlox subulata*
'Magenta'   p.47

Middle: *Polygonum affine*
'Superbum'   p.47

Bottom: *Potentilla alba*   p.48

of weed development by the unavoidable soil disturbance during planting can be minimised by mulching disturbed areas with peat or other weed-free mulches. Similarly it is beneficial to mulch the exposed areas between newly-planted ground-covers to suppress weeds until the plants meet to give continuous cover; alternatively, regular hand-weeding with minimal disturbance will enable the ground-cover plants to become established, unhindered by competition.

Maintenance of ground-cover

Lush growth is generally not desirable for ground-cover plants, but a spring application of general fertilizer or bone meal may be needed to prevent thinning of the cover or dying-out. Where plants cover the ground without extensive rooting down it is possible to raise the trailing shoots and apply the fertilizer to the soil around the base of the plant. This is not possible for plants such as thyme or *Cotula* which form a closely rooted mat. In such cases liquid foliar feeds could be applied during late spring or early summer.

Limited trimming or pruning of ground-cover plants may be needed to keep them tidy and to prevent the more vigorous ones from swamping other plants. Some such as *Cotula* and prostrate thymes need no trimming, but those of more bushy habit can be cut back lightly with shears after flowering. Woody plants such as ericas should be trimmed regularly to retain a bushy form and to prevent them becoming thin and straggly.

7 A SELECTION OF WEED – SUPPRESSING GROUND – COVER PLANTS

The plants described in this chapter inevitably reflect the likes and dislikes of the authors, and their perception of what constitutes a ground-cover plant. However most, but not all, of the plants described are also included in the more extensive list published in the RHS Wisley Handbook on 'Ground Cover Plants'.

The brief descriptions of some of the selected species are supplemented by photographs. Heights (in cm) generally refer to the vegetative parts; where flower spikes etc. rise appreciably above the level of the foliage, their height is indicated separately. The spread of the plants is not given as the time taken to achieve the maximum spread is very variable. The planting spacing suggested should give complete ground-cover within 1 - 2 years under good growing conditions using healthy, good-quality planting material. Slow-growing plants should be planted at a closer spacing than rapidly-growing ones, even though an isolated slow-growing plant might eventually spread further than an isolated rapidly-growing one.

Each species is also given a 'Type' number, corresponding to the growth form types shown in Fig 6. and discussed in chapter 6. This information is helpful in the planning of plant groupings for visual impact as well as for weed management, but in addition gives an indication of the methods of propagation and the possibilities for rapid and economical multiplication of plants for extensive planting.

Acaena (Rosaceae) – Bidibidis:
Acaena buchananii: From New Zealand providing a rapidly-spreading light blue-green 'carpet' 4-5 cm. high. The flowers are insignificant. Excellent over small bulbs.
Planting distance: 50cm.   (Type 2)

35

Acaena microphylla: Another continually-rooting mat-forming plant from New Zealand. It spreads rapidly, but is only 6-10cm high and requires a sunny well drained site. The flowers are inconspicuous but give rise to attractive scarlet-spined burrs. (Plate 1).
Planting distance: 30cm. (Type 2)

Ajuga reptans (Labiatae) – Bugle: The many cultivars are selected forms of the native British species, spreading moderately rapidly by creeping stems that root down at frequent intervals to give a prostrate mat 5-10cm high, with erect spikes of blue flowers 20-25cm. Some cultivars have strongly coloured foliage, 'Atropurpurea' – reddish purple, 'Burgundy Glow' – purple, bronze and gold patterns, and 'Variegata' – silver and green. Bugles flourish in most soils, best in partial shade but are tolerant of full shade. However, red-leaved forms are more deeply coloured in sunny conditions. (Plate 1).
Planting distance: 20-30cm. (Type 3)

Alchemilla mollis (Rosaceae) – Lady's Mantle: A herbaceous plant originating in the Carpathian Mountains and Turkey, forming spreading clumps of pale green, hairy, palmately lobed leaves with toothed edges, 30-40cm high. The rather insignificant yellow-green flowers are borne in clusters carried above the leaves. The plant dies down completely in the winter, but forms a dense cover during the growing season.
Planting distance: 30-40cm. (Type 4)

Antennaria dioica (Compositae) – Catsfoot: A plant of heaths , moors and mountain grasslands in Europe, Asia and N.America. The leaves, on prostrate readily-rooting stems, are green on the upper surface but have a grey-white woolly under-surface. The plant spreads rather slowly, forming a mat 2-4cm high, with erect flower stalks (about 6cm) carrying small heads of flowers, deep pink in the cultivar 'Rosea' but variable – often much paler – in the wild. Needs a sunny position and gives a good cover over small bulbs.
Planting distance: 20-25cm. (Type 2)

Asarum europaeum (Aristolochiaceae) – **Asasabacca**: A native of southern Europe, in woods on calcareous soils. Shiny deep-green kidney-shaped leaves on long stalks arise from fairly slowly spreading underground stems (rhizomes), height 8-10cm. Flowers are inconspicuous purple-brown bells concealed below the leaves. Excellent ground-cover in moist and shady conditions. (Plate 1).
Planting distance: 20-30cm.   (Type 3)

Aubrieta deltoidea (Cruciferae) – **Aubrietia**: From the European Mediterranean area, Sicily to Turkey. A wide range of cultivars with long trailing stems, hairy wedge-shaped, coarsely toothed leaves, and white, pink or purple flowers in early spring. Stems root down only if covered with soil or compost, and should be trimmed back hard after flowering. Best in a sunny position on calcareous soils, forming hummocks 7-10cm high.
Planting distance: 25-30cm.   (Type 1a)

Azorella trifurcata (= *Bolax glebaria*) (**Umbelliferae**): Native in Chile and the Falkland Islands. Forms slowly-expanding hummocks consisting of close-packed rosettes of hard, leathery and somewhat 'spikey' leaves. Insignificant and short-lived yellowish flowers arise in small groups from the centre of the rosettes. Tolerates stony ground in sunny positions. The rosettes are 2-3cm high, but long-established hummocks in the wild may build up to form a hard cushion 60cm or more in height.
Planting distance: 20cm.   (Type 1b)

Bergenia **species & hybrids** (Saxifragaceae): Various species originated in Siberia, China, the Himalayas and Afghanistan. The cultivated forms are mostly large-leaved evergreen plants, ranging from 20-30cm high, with large heads of bell-shaped white,pink or purple flowers appearing between January and April.
Planting distance: 20-60cm.   (Type 1c)

Calluna vulgaris (Ericaceae) – **Heather, Ling**: A native of N.W.Europe, with numerous cultivars, all requiring acid (non-calcareous) soils. Forms gradually-spreading hummocks ranging in height and spread from 15cm to 60cm. A choice can be made from cultivars with green, grey, orange, red or yellow foliage with white, pink or purple flowers from July to November.
Planting distance: 20-45cm.   (Type 1c)

Campanula poscharskyana (Campanulaceae): A plant of eastern European origin, forming dense tangled mats of long prostrate stems and small, rounded heart-shaped leaves with rounded teeth, spreading also by extensive underground stems. The leafy carpet, 8-10cm high, is covered in June and July with lavender-blue star-like flowers. Somewhat invasive, but excellent in areas of poor soil, and will 'fill in' the base of a *Thuja* or *Cupressus* hedge that has become sparse and open, and will climb to about 30cm around the base of a tree or up a wall. Needs to be pulled out vigourously at the end of the season, but soon develops fresh leaf cover which persists through the winter. (Plate 2). Planting distance: 30-40cm. (Type 3)

Cerastium tomentosum (Caryophyllaceae) – Snow-in-summer: A carpet-forming 'evergreen' species 10-15cm high with woolly silver-grey foliage and starry white flowers in profusion in early summer. It roots down extensively and can become invasive and suppress other small plants. Requires full sun and tolerates dry conditions on banks and rockeries.
Planting distance: 35cm. (Type 2)

Ceratostigma plumbaginoides (Plumbaginaceae): This Chinese herbaceous species spreads by underground suckers and in early summer produces a dense clump of 20cm high wiry stems carrying small green leaves. Bright blue flowers start to open in July and continue until November, and during this time the leaves develop an attractive deep red colouration. Requires a sunny, well-drained site.
Planting distance: 30-40cm. (Type 3)

Cornus canadensis (Cornaceae) – Creeping dogwood: Native of North America, requiring lime-free soil and cool moist conditions, and tolerating some shade. Underground runners throw up shoots with deciduous rounded leathery dark-green leaves, forming a dense carpet 10-15cm high. Each cluster of small inconspicuous flowers is surrounded by four large white bracts, and gives rise to a group of bright red berries.
Planting distance: 30-40cm. (Type 3)

Cotoneaster species (Rosaceae): Several prostrate and hummock-forming forms carrying bright red berries in autumn make effective ground-cover plants, most of which have been introduced from China.

Cotoneaster congestus: A slow-growing evergreen with crowded shoots forming a dense mat 8-10cm high, rooting down at intervals.
Planting distance: 30cm. (Type 2)

Cotoneaster dammeri: Evergreen spreading plants slowly building up to form a dense mat, 8-10cm high. (Plate 2).
Planting distance: 25cm. (Type 2)

Cotoneaster 'Gnome': Forms a dense evergreen carpet 8-10cm high, but covers the ground more rapidly than *C.congestus.*
Planting distance: 50cm. (Type 2)

Cotoneaster horizontalis: A deciduous species which roots down sparsely; its 'herring bone' form and relatively rapid growth make it an effective ground-cover, especially on a bank, where it tends to spread upwards and remain fairly flat rather than building up into hummocks.
Planting distance: 100cm. (Type 1a)

Cotoneaster microphyllus: Densely growing evergreen plants which rapidly build up into hummocks 30-45cm high.
Planting distance 100cm. (Type 1b)

Cotula squalida (Compositae): A native from New Zealand, this is a low-growing (2-3cm) densely-carpeting ground-cover plant, which can become invasive. The flowers are greenish-yellow and insignificant, but the deeply pinnate bronze-green leaves, arising from creeping and continually rooting stems, are very attractive. The leaves die and turn brown during winter, and sometimes also under drought conditions in summer, but new leaves emerge rapidly as soon as growing conditions improve. It is an excellent cover for dwarf spring- and autumn-flowering 'bulbs', and is happy in light shade. (Plate 2).
Planting distance: 20-25cm. (Type 3)

Dryas octopetala (Rosaceae) – **Mountain avens:** A circumpolar mountain species, which grows wild in the UK, requiring full sun and well-drained or stony soil. A rather slow-growing evergreen plant with prostrate woody stems and dark green glossy leaves with white woolly

39

undersides, shaped like miniature oak-leaves. It forms a mat 3-5cm high, rooting down to a limited extent. White 8-petalled solitary flowers are carried on erect stalks well above the leaves.
Planting distance: 25-35cm.   (Type 2)

Erica (Ericaceae) – **Heaths:** From the mountain areas of Europe. Many species and cultivars of evergreen hardy shrubs and sub-shrubs are included in the genus *Erica*. (Plate 3).
  Erica cinerea – **Bell heather:** Requires an acidic soil, cultivars growing 10-30cm high with white, lilac or pink flowers from June to October.
Planting distance: 20-30cm.   (Type 1c)
  Erica x darleyensis (E.herbacea x E.erigena): Cultivars are lime-tolerant, 25-50cm high, and have winter flowers in a wide range of colours, from white to deep pink and purple.
Planting distance: 40-50cm.   (Type 1c)
  Erica erigena: Lime-tolerant winter-flowering cultivars, 30-70cm high, with a wide range of flower colours, white,pink and purple, and forming dense ground-cover.
Planting distance: 25-35cm.   (Type 1c)
  Erica herbacea (= *E.carnea*): A widely grown species that will tolerate neutral or calcareous soils. Cultivars vary in height, up to 25cm, with white or pink flowers appearing from November to May, and have green, red-bronze or yellow leaves; some are more or less prostrate, others are more erect in form. They spread moderately slowly, but eventually make a dense ground-cover.
Planting distance: 30-40cm.   (Type 1c)
  Erica tetralix – **Cross-leaved heather:** Foliage grows from 15-30cm, and makes an effective ground-cover on acid soils, with white, pink or crimson flowers from June to August.
Planting distance: 20-30cm.   (Type 1c)

Euphorbia (Euphorbiaceae) – **spurges**
  Euphorbia amygdaloides var. *robbiae:* A native of Turkey, this evergreen species, about 35cm in height, develops a spreading network of underground stems, and a succession of erect shoots bearing dark green leathery leaves. The leaves persist through the winter and the shoots extend rapidly in the spring to form spikes of small flowers

with prominent yellow-green bracts. Shoots that will flower in the following year develop during the summer, whilst those that have already flowered die down. It is tolerant of shade and has no special soil requirements. (Plate 3).

Planting distance: 50cm. (Type 3)

Euphorbia cyparissias: A herbaceous European species, forms effective ground-cover, but can be invasive. The shoots are 25-30cm, are densely clothed with narrow light-green leaves and at the top have clusters of flowers with greenish-yellow bracts, which develop a reddish coloration as the seeds mature.

Planting distance: 40cm. (Type 3)

Gaultheria procumbens (Ericaceae) – **Partridge berry:** Native of the north-east of N.America. Creeping, underground stems give rise to shoots with shiny dark-green leaves, forming a dense cover about 15cm high. Clusters of small white or pink bell-shaped flowers are followed by bright red berries. Requires acid (non-calcareous) soils, and grows well in shade. (Plate 3).

Planting distance: 30-40cm. (Type 3)

Genista hispanica (**Leguminosae**) – **Spanish gorse:** Originating in S.W. Europe, this hummock-forming plant requires a sunny well-drained position. Although deciduous, with narrow needle-like leaves, the stems and spines are also green, giving a persistent green effect during the winter. Bright yellow flowers appear in clusters at the end of the new shoots in June and July. Moderately slow-growing, to a height and spread of about 60cm eventually.

Planting distance: 50cm. (Type 1b)

Geranium (Geraniaceae) – Crane's bills:

Geranium cinereum subcaulescens: A Balkan species, forms a relatively low and spreading ground-cover, 10-15cm high, with creeping stems that root down, black-centered bright magenta flowers, and rounded lobed grey-green leaves.

Planting distance: 30cm. (Type 2)

Geranium endressii: This Western Pyreneean species forms dense clumps of attractive foliage – 30-50cm high – and provides excellent ground-cover. Pale pink flowers, lightly veined in red, are produced from May to August. Several cultivars and hybrids are available. It is tolerant of light shade.

Planting distance: 30cm.   (Type 4)

Geranium himalayense (= *G. grandiflorum*): A spreading bushy species, 30cm high, with deep blue flowers appearing in June and July.

Planting distance: 30cm.   (Type 4)

Geranium x Johnson's Blue (*G. himalayense* x *G.pratense*): A spreading bushy hybrid. 30cm high with pale blue flowers in July.

Planting distance 30cm.   (Type 4)

Geranium x magnificum (= *G. ibericum*): This bushy hybrid will thrive in a hot sunny position, growing to 30cm, and produces violet-blue flowers in August.

Planting distance: 30cm.   (Type 4)

Geranium renardii: A compact bushy plant with grey-green leaves and pale lavender-white flowers with purple markings from May until July.

Planting distance: 25cm.   (Type 1b)

Geranium sanguineum – **Bloody crane's bill:** A species native to Europe, (including the UK). Spreads by creeping underground stems, from which arise mid-green deeply lobed leaves, and from June to September, crimson-magenta flowers. Height 15-25cm, covering the ground fairly rapidly. (Plate 4).

Planting distance: 40cm.   (Type 3)

Geranium sanguineum lancastriense: A dwarf form 8-10cm high, with pale pink flowers, which is also a satisfactory ground-cover plant, but requires closer spacing to achieve rapid cover.

Planting distance: 30cm.   (Type 3)

Geranium sylvaticum: A European shade-tolerant species with white or lavender-blue flowers in May and June. It forms clumps about 30-40cm high with silvery-green leaves.

Planting distance: 35cm.   (Type 1b)

Hacquetia epipactis (**Umbelliferae**): A European alpine species. Creeping stems give rise to tufts of rounded 3-lobed toothed leaves and flowerstalks bearing tight clusters of small yellow flowers in April-May, each cluster surrounded by 5-6 relatively large leafy bracts. Height 8-15cm, fairly slow growing and tolerant of shade. (Plate 4).

Planting distance: 15-20cm.   (Type 3)

Hebe (Scrophulariaceae) – Shrubby veronicas:
These evergreen flowering shrubs, predominantly of New Zealand origin, have neat dense foliage making the hardy cultivars good ground-cover plants suitable for use in various weed-suppressing groupings. Many produce attractive flowers over a long period. Growth is best in full sun on well-drained soil.

Hebe 'Pewter Dome': Forms a hummock up to 60cm, with grey-green foliage and numerous 5cm spikes of white flowers.
Planting distance: 60cm.   (Type 1b)
Hebe pinguifolia 'Pagei': A spreading plant, 15-25cm high, also with glaucous grey foliage and white flowers. (Plate 4).
Planting distance: 40cm.   (Type 2)
Hebe 'Carl Teschner': A spreading plant, up to 30cm high, with violet-blue flowers in June and July.
Planting distance: 25cm.   (Type 2)
Hebe 'Great Orme': An upright bushy plant (to 120cm) with pink flowers Planting distance: 60cm.   (Type 1b)

Hedera helix (Araliaceae) - Ivy: Many of the numerous cultivars of this evergreen native species are excellent ground-cover plants, the long trailing stems rooting down wherever they touch the soil. There are wide ranges of variation in the size, shape and colour variegation of the leaves, and in growth rate. Some will form a 'mat' about 15cm deep, others will build up to 30cm or more. Ivies generally do not flower whilst their shoots are growing horizontally, and remain in their characteristic juvenile 'ivy-leaf' form. After climbing to the top of an upright support they commonly develop larger leaves, which are not lobed, and produce flowers and eventually fruits. Cuttings taken from these shoots retain the 'adult' type of foliage and tend to form bushy freely-flowering shrubs rather than reverting to the postrate trailing form. As ground-cover the ivies are shade tolerant, but the degree of shading may affect the colour of some variegated forms, especially where there is some pinkish colouration.
Planting distance: 60-100cm, depending on vigour.   (Type 2)

Helianthemum nummularium (Cistaceae) – Rock-roses: Occurs in the wild throughout Europe (including the UK) in grassy and rocky places, especially on limestone and chalk, where it is mainly yellow flowered. The numerous cultivars, 10-15cm high, mostly with grey-green leaves retained through the winter, may be single or double flowered in a wide range of colours – yellow, orange, scarlet, white etc. Single forms close but double forms remain open when the sun is not shining. They require well-drained soil and full sun to produce a dense cover, and should be cut back after flowering to maintain a compact form.

Planting distance: 15-20cm. (Type 1c)

Hosta (Liliaceae) – Plantain lilies: Cultivars of a number of the Japanese species are hardy clump-forming herbaceous shade-tolerant perennials which form effective summer ground-cover, ranging in height from 30-100cm. The leaves, stalked and generally ovate or heart-shaped, are strongly veined and vary in colour from a glaucous blue-green to yellowish-green, and may be edged with 'gold' or 'silver', or more extensively variegated. Tall spikes of flowers, light blue to violet-mauve, appear in July and August. Hostas are leafless during the winter and can be interplanted with spring-flowering bulbs (daffodils, narcissi etc). As the leaves of the bulbs become senescent they are covered by the developing foliage of the hostas.

Hosta crispula: has narrow pointed leaves with white margins, giving clumps 30cm high.
Planting distance: 40cm. (Type 4)
Hosta elata: Dense green foliage forms a clump 45cm in height.
Planting distance: 45cm. (Type 4)
Hosta fortunei: Cultivars have variegated leaves which grow into wide clumps up to 45cm high. (Plate 5).
Planting distance: 50cm. (Type 4)
Hosta sieboldiana: Cultivars have large blue-grey or grey-green leaves forming 45cm high clumps.
Planting distance: 50cm. (Type 4)

Houttuynia cordata (Saururaceae): From China and Japan. Erect red stems, 30-40cm high, with blue-green heart-shaped leaves arise from underground runners. Close-packed conical clusters of small inconspicuous flowers are borne at the centre of groups of four petal-like white bracts at the tips of the shoots. In the cultivar *H. cordata* 'Flore Pleno' the white bracts are more numerous. This species flourishes in

cool moist conditions, and even in wet soil or shallow water, and will tolerate light shade. It can sometimes become invasive. (Plate 5). There are several variegated forms including 'Chameleon', with multi-coloured leaves.
Planting distance: 20-30cm. (Type 3)

Hypericum (Guttiferae)
Hypericum calycinum – **Rose of Sharon, St John's Wort:**
A native of S.E.Europe and W.Turkey. A dense carpet of erect shoots, 20-30cm high, arises from a rapidly spreading mat of underground stems. The large golden-yellow flowers with massed stamens are carried, mostly singly, at the tips of the shoots. This plant is tolerant of shade and will grow almost anywhere. It should be cut back drastically each spring to maintain maximum density of cover,
Planting distance: 40-50cm. (Type 3)
Hypericum cerastoides (= *H. rhodopeum*): From Turkey and the Balkans. Semi-recumbent shoots, 8-10cm long, carrying grey-green foliage and large yellow flowers, tend to root down and form a carpet. This species requires full sun and a well-drained soil.
Planting distance: 20-30cm. (Type 2)

Iberis sempervirens (Cruciferae): Native of southern Europe. This bushy hummock-forming evergreen plant, 20-30cm high, has dark green leaves, and flat heads of white flowers in early summer. The cultivar 'Snowflake' is a compact and dense form. Sunny and well-drained conditions are required.
Planting distance: 30-40cm. (Type 1b)

Juniperus species (Cupressaceae) – **Junipers:** Evergreen coniferous species of naturally prostrate habit, and prostrate cultivars of species that are usually erect trees or shrubs can be valuable ground-cover plants.
Juniperus communis – **Common juniper:** From north temperate regions, is typically a 3m high bush, but various dwarf and prostrate cultivars and varieties are available, e.g. *J. communis* var. jackii, a prostrate variety from the Rocky Mountains, 15-20cm high, occasionally rooting down.
Planting distance: 60cm. (Type 1a)

Juniperus horizontalis: A prostrate species from N.E.America, grows only 15-25cm high but spreads eventually up to 2m wide. Cultivars are available with glaucous, green or bronze foliage. Branches in contact with the soil often root down. The cultivar Bar Harbor has glaucous grey-green leaves.

Planting distance: 45-60cm.   (Type 1a)

Juniperus squamata: An Asian species which is extremely variable in growth form. The cultivar Blue Star forms a dense low-growing bush with silvery-blue foliage, excellent in groupings with heaths and heathers. Roots down only occasionally. (Plate 3)

Planting distance: 50cm.   (Type 1a)

Lamiastrum galeobdolon (= *Lamium galeobdolon,* = *Galeobdolon argentatum*) (Labiatae) – Yellow archangel: A rampant ground-cover, up to 50cm tall, with silver-marbled leaves, persisting through the winter, and whorls of yellow 'dead nettle' flowers. Tolerant of shade and useful under trees or large shrubs, but not suitable among small plants.

Planting distance: 40-50cm.   (Type 2)

Lamium maculatum (Labiatae) – Spotted dead nettle: A species introduced into Britain but native in much of Europe and western Asia. Although a herbaceous plant, 8-10cm high and spreading by underground stems, the leaves with their characteristic central silver stripe are retained throughout the winter. Spikes of purplish-pink flowers appear in spring, as early as mid-March after a mild winter, and continue to be produced for many weeks. There is also a white variety *L.maculatum album.* Both forms grow well in most soils and will tolerate shade. They should be trimmed with shears after flowering, to ensure a continuous dense leaf-cover.

Planting distance: 30-40cm.   (Type 3)

Lithodora diffusa (= *Lithospermum diffusum*) (Boraginaceae): A hairy evergreen southern European plant, with spreading prostrate stems, small dark green leaves and blue flowers forming a dense mat, 10-20cm high. It requires a sunny position and does not tolerate calcareous soils. The cultivars most commonly available are 'Heavenly Blue' and 'Grace Ward'. The stems generally do not root down unless covered with peat or soil.

Planting distance: 30-40cm.   (Type 1a)

Lonicera pileata (Caprifoliaceae): This species from China forms a dense spreading bush 60-90cm high. It is normally evergreen, but may lose many of its leaves in a severe winter. The inconspicuous greenish-yellow flowers are borne on the underside of the shoots in April and May and are followed by purplish berries. Shoots in contact with soil root down, and they form an excellent ground-cover on banks or other inaccessible places, although they may have to be restrained by clipping.
Planting distance: 60-75cm.   (Type 1b)

Maianthemum bifolium (Liliaceae) – **May lily:** A European and Asian woodland plant, spreading by creeping underground stems, from which arise flowering shoots, 10-15cm high, each carrying two shiny heart-shaped leaves and a spike of small white flowers with prominent stamens, from May until July. The fruit is a red berry. This plant requires a leafy soil and some shade.
Planting distance: 30-40cm.   (Type 3)

Pachysandra terminalis (Buxaceae): A semi-woody evergreen plant from Japan, up to 30cm high, spreading by underground stems, and providing good cover under dry shady conditions, e.g. under trees. The insignificant flowers develop in small spikes, and have large prominent white stamens. (Plate 5).
Planting distance: 25-30cm.   (Type 3)

Phlox subulata (Polemoniaceae) – **Moss phlox:** From the eastern United States. Spreading mats of narrow mid-green leaves, stems rooting down, and producing masses of short-stemmed flowers over the whole mat in early summer. A wide range of cultivars is available with colours ranging from white, pale pink and pale mauve to brilliant magenta-red, 5-10 cm high. Needs a well-drained soil in full sun. (Plate 6).
Planting distance: 20-30cm.   (Type 3)

Polygonum (Polygonaceae) – **Knotweeds:**
   Polygonum affine: A native of Nepal which forms a close mat of narrow, dark-green leaves, 5-10cm high, spreading by creeping stems that rapidly root down. Spikes, 15-20cm, of small pink flowers appear from July to September. The cultivars Darjeeling Red and Superbum are recommended for ground-cover. Their foliage turns a foxy red

and remains throughout the winter, until gradually replaced by new leaves in the spring. Best in a sunny position. (Plate 6).
Planting distance: 20-30cm.   (Type 2)

Polygonum vacciniifolium: This Himalayan species produces elegant tapering spikes of pink flowers in September and October, over a dense mat of shining deep-green elliptic leaves. Once established it spreads fairly rapidly, rooting down where the shoots are in contact with the soil. Height 8-10cm, requires a sunny position. The leaves are lost during the winter, but the brown matted stems persist, and produce new leaves in the spring.
Planting distance: 20-30cm.   (Type 2)

Potentilla (Rosaceae) – Cinquefoils:
Potentilla alba – White cinquefoil: A herbaceous perennial from central and eastern Europe. Leaves deeply 5-lobed, green above and silvery below, on creeping stems that root down continually, forming a dense carpet with white flowers on stems 5-8cm high. It will tolerate some light shade and makes an excellent combined planting with autumn flowering crocuses. (Plate 6).
Planting distance: 20-30cm.   (Type 2)
Potentilla fruticosa – Shrubby cinquefoil: This species is widespread in the northern hemisphere, forming a much-branched deciduous shrub up to 100cm high, with greyish pinnate leves and clusters of yellow flowers. Some cultivars form dense hummocks, 40-50cm high. Needs a sunny position on any well-drained soil.
Planting distance: 60-75cm.   (Type 1c)

Prunella grandiflora (Labiatae) – Self-heal: Occurs wild throughout Europe, in grassy places colonising any bare ground. Cultivated forms give a dense ground-cover, 8-10cm high, spreading by creeping stems that root down readily and can become invasive. Dense, 15cm, spikes of 'dead-nettle' flowers, pink, mauve or purple-violet, are produced throughout the summer. It is favoured by fairly moist conditions and does well in shade.
Planting distance: 30cm.   (Type 3)

PLATE SEVEN:

PLATE EIGHT:

Top: *Thymus serpyllum lanuginosus* (left) and *Thymus serpyllum coccineus*   p.51

Middle: *Vinca minor* 'Burgundy'   p.52

Bottom: *Waldsteinia ternata*   p.53

Pulmonaria (Boraginaceae) – Lungworts:
Native European herbaceous clump-forming plants, 10-20cm high.
Planting distance 30cm.   (Type 4)
   Pulmonaria angustifolia: Unspotted leaves and blue flowers, dying
   back to a small rosette in winter.
   Pulmonaria officinalis: White-spotted leaves, and flowers that open
   pink and then turn blue; leaves are often retained during the winter.
   (Plate 7).
   Pulmonaria rubra: Rather pale leaves, practically evergreen, and
   pinkish-red flowers.

Raoulia australis (Compositae) – Scabweed or Mat Daisy: This New
Zealand alpine forms thin encrusting mats, typically in stony locations.
Closely packed grey shoots, up to 5mm high, with minute heads of
yellow flowers in late summer. An attractive 'ground-cover' in small-
scale plantings, e.g. amongst alpines in rock-gardens or troughs, but
not reliably hardy.
Planting distance 10cm.   (Type 2)

Rhododendron species and hybrids (Ericaceae):
Predominantly from the Himalayas, China, Tibet etc; virtually all require
acid (non-calcaeous) soils and are essentially woodland plants, mostly
evergreen. Where they can be used they form very effective weed-
suppressing ground-cover, their dense leathery foliage excludes light
from the soil whilst on the plant, and after it is shed, decomposes to
form a deep persistent mulch. The range of species and cultivars is so
wide that is not practicable to make specific recommendations for
ground-cover.
                                                            (Type 1b)

Rosa species and hybrids (Rosaceae) – Roses: Although some 'species'
roses will form a fairly dense bush, e.g. *Rosa rugosa, R.rubrifolia, R.xanthina*
'Canary Bird', they are of limited value as weed-suppressing ground-
cover. However certain prostrate roses can be used where a substantial
area of ground is to be covered.
   Rosa wichuraiana: Spreads to form a dense carpet, 3m in diameter, with
   single white flowers. The cultivar Max Graf, a hybrid between
   R.wichuraiana and *R.rugosa,* is also a prostrate ground-covering form,

with large pink single flowers produced over a long period from late June. (Plate 7). 'Temple Bells' is an R.H.S.-recommended cultivar giving full ground-cover in two seasons.
Planting distance: 90-120cm.   (Type 5)

Saxifraga (Saxifragaceae) – saxifrages:
Saxifraga – **mossy species:** These make good ground-cover although their evergreen rosettes are smaller than those of *S.* x *urbium* and their shorter flower stalks carry one or a few larger cup-shaped flowers. They need a sunny well-drained site, but sometimes die out in patches for no obvious reason.
Saxifraga x urbium – **London pride:** An evergreen hybrid between *S. umbrosa* and *S.spathularis*, forming dark green rosettes of rather fleshy leaves, 5-8cm high, with erect flower stalks up to 30cm, carrying panicles of small pink star-shaped flowers. Fairly tolerant of shade.
Planting distance: 30cm.   (Type 3)

Sedum spurium **(Crassulaceae):** Native of the Caucasus and northern Iran. A mat-forming evergreen succulent plant 5-10cm high, with dense flattened heads of pink flowers in July and August. It spreads by creeping and rooting stems which give rise to rosettes of fleshy leaves. The cultivar Green Mantle is a non-flowering form, making a dense carpet.
Planting distance: 20-30cm.   (Type 3)

Skimmia **(Rutaceae):** Hardy evergreen slow-growing shrubs bearing male and female flowers on separate plants in March and April. They will tolerate some shade when planted on well-drained soils.
Planting distance: 50-60cm.   (Type 1b)
Skimmia japonica: From Japan, one of the larger species which can grow to 45-90cm in height. The creamy-white flowers on the female plants develop into bright red persistent berries, ripening in August and September. (Plate 7). The cultivar Bowles' Dwarf reaches only 30cm and forms a dense carpet that rarely produces flowers. *S.* x 'Formanii' resembles *S. japonica* and has fragrant female flowers followed by particularly brilliant red berries.
Skimmia reevesiana (= *S. fortunei*): A Chinese species forming a hummock eventually reaching 45-90cm high. The creamy-white

flowers in dense panicles appear in spring followed by crimson fruits on the female plants. The cultivar 'Rubella' is a male form which has crimson flower buds.

Thymus (Labiatae) – **Thyme:** Numerous species and cultivars are available for use as evergreen ground-cover. They very greatly in growth form, height (2-15cm), colour of foliage and flowers and time of flowering. The compact prostrate forms require virtually no maintenance but the more erect forms need to be trimmed with shears after flowering. All do best in a sunny well-drained position, and often spread over rocks, walls, paving stones etc, rooting down wherever the opportunity arises. Planting distance: 20cm.   (Type 2)
  Thymus 'Pink Chintz': Is a low growing form about 5cm producing many large deep pink flowers.
  Thymus serpyllum: Has a number of subspecies and cultivars.
  Thymus serpyllum albus: Is a prostrate white flowered form with deep green foliage.
  Thymus serpyllum coccineus: Is another prostrate form, 5cm high, with dark green foliage and deep crimson buds opening to pink flowers. (Plate 8). The cultivar Minor has similar flowers but is only 2cm high.
  Thymus serpyllum lanuginosus: Has very attractive grey woolly foliage, 5cm in height, and pale pink flowers. (Plate 8).

Tiarella cordifolia (Saxifragaceae): A North American species, spreading by surface runners that give rise to light-green palmately-lobed leaves, which form a dense evergreen ground-cover 8-10cm high. Erect spikes of small creamy white flowers, up to 25cm high, appear in early summer. It grows well in shade, especially where there are leaves rotting under trees.
Planting distance: 30-40cm.   (Type 3)

Veronica prostrata (Scrophulariaceae): Occurs wild in Europe and northern Asia. A prostrate mat-forming species, rooting down continually as the creeping stems advance; usually only 2-5cm high. The flowers are deep blue in the wild type, but cultivars are available with pale blue and pink flowers.
Planting distance: 20-30cm.   (Type 2)

Vinca (Apocynaceae) – **Periwinkles:** Evergreen European shade tolerant plants which make very effective ground-cover under trees, flowering in winter, spring and summer. They have no special soil requirements other than reasonably good drainage.

Vinca major – **Greater periwinkle:** This is a vigorous species, 15-20cm in height, with deep blue flowers. The long arching fast-growing shoots root down at their tips and often prove too invasive for small gardens.

Planting distance: 45cm.   (Type 2)

Vinca minor – **Lesser periwinkle:** This smaller species, 10-15cm in height, roots down at every 'joint' and soon forms a tight mat of foliage. The wild form has blue flowers but there are also selected cultivars with white, wine-red, blue-purple and plum-purple flowers. Forms with variegated foliage, somewhat less vigorous, are also available. (Plate 8).

Planting distance: 35-40cm.   (Type 2)

Viola (Violaceae) – **Violets:**

Viola cornuta: From the Pyrenees and Alps. A long flowering species which spreads by creeping stems which root down frequently, 8-10cm in height. The wild form has deep purple flowers but there are cultivars with paler coloured and also white flowers. Does well in cool well-drained soils that do not get too dry.

Planting distance: 25-30cm.   (Type 2)

Viola **'Huntercombe Purple':** Gives a very dense cover 8-10cm high carrying deep purple flowers.

Planting distance: 25-30cm.   (Type 2)

Viola labradorica: Purple-flushed foliage develops from freely running underground stems. It gives a very dense cover in sun or shade but can be invasive. Mauve flowers in April and May.

Planting distance: 25-30cm.   (Type 3)

Viola septentrionalis: From eastern North America. This is a deciduous species, the leaves dying down completely in the winter. However, growth begins early in the summer from substantial underground rhizomes, and rapidly develops a dense leafy cover, 10-15cm high, which suppresses all seedling weeds. The form ***Viola septentrionalis alba*** has exceptionally beautiful flowers, white, with dark purple veining of the petals; the wild violet-blue form is less

striking, but is an equally effective ground-cover. The plant spreads by underground stems.
Planting distance: 25-30cm.   (Type 3)

Waldesteinia ternata **(Rosaceae)**: From Japan and Siberia. An evergreen, 8-10cm high, that spreads by readily-rooting creeping stems. It grows well in moist or dry soils, in sun or shade, producing yellow flowers resembling those of strawberries through the summer months. (Plate 8). Planting distance: 30cm.   (Type 2)

ADDITIONAL INFORMATION

The following publications contain much useful information on ground-cover plants:

Ground Cover Plants by Margery Fish (Faber Paperbacks).
Plants for Ground Cover by Graham Stuart Thomas (Dent).
Ground Cover Plants A Wisley Handbook (Cassell).

8 MANAGING WITHOUT WEEDS

Cultivation, herbicides, mulches, ground-cover plants all have a role in controlling weeds, but they differ in what they do most efficiently, and none on its own will provide an effective method of control that is simultaneously labour saving, time saving, environment saving, and visually acceptable in the garden. By combining different methods it is possible to use each one for the job that it does best: cultivation for preparing the soil for planting, and stimulating weeds into growth; systemic herbicides for eliminating perennial (and annual) weeds; long-persisting residual herbicides for preventing all plant growth on footpaths, at the base of fences etc.; weed-free mulches for suppressing the growth of weed-seedlings, by excluding the light from exposed soil from which perennial weeds have been eliminated, while allowing the growth of established perennial plants, and of spring and autumn bulbs etc.; and ground-cover plants, having a similar effect to mulches, but competing with seedling weeds for water and nutrients as well as excluding light, eventually giving complete cover and generally being 'self-renewing' from year to year with minimal maintenance.

The basic sequence of operations is therefore as follows:

(1) Prepare the soil by cultivation, incorporating organic or other fertilizers as required by digging, forking, hoeing etc., in autumn or spring.

(2) Await a flush of vigorous weed growth, then apply a systemic herbicide, e.g. glyphosate, being careful to avoid any valuable plants nearby. After 3 weeks, cultivate shallowly, e.g. with a tined cultivator, to stimulate the next flush of weed seedlings and any persistent established perennial weeds (Nettles, docks, thistles, couch grass, ground elder, etc.). When these are growing vigorously, spray again with glyphosate. After another three or four weeks, cultivate shallowly again. A third application of glyphosate may be necessary to eliminate finally any residual couch grass and other perennial weeds. After this the soil should not be disturbed more than is necessary for planting up.

(3) After planting, all exposed soil should be covered with a weed-free mulch to suppress any new weed seedling growth.
(4) If ground-cover plants are being used, they should be planted at relatively close spacing (as indicated in the chapter on ground-cover plants) to achieve complete cover in 1-2 years. Meanwhile, weed-free mulches should be used to cover exposed soil between the plants.

This complete schedule is mainly applicable for permanent ornamental plantings, with trees, shrubs, herbaceous perennials etc. It can nevertheless be applied **in part** for displays of bedding plants, the preparation of new lawns, and in vegetable gardens. The initial preparations (1) and (2) above, will drastically reduce weed populations of vegetable plots, flower beds, and sites for lawns, and the use of weed-free mulches will supress further weed development amongst bedding plants until the planting becomes dense enough to provide its own ground-cover. In the vegetable garden the use of weed-free mulches would be beneficial but probably not economic, except perhaps for plants that remain in position for several months. However there is considerable scope for experimenting with black polythene, and the newer water-permeable sheetings, either planting through slits in continuous sheets for spaced plants such as brassicas, strawberries etc., or placing strips between the rows of crops such as carrots, onions, broad beans, peas, etc. However, even if one decides to rely on hoeing to control weeds in vegetables, the preparation treatments (1) and (2) will still greatly reduce the initial weed population and make control by cultivation less arduous.

Whatever combination of methods is finally adopted in the garden, it is important that the operations should be carried out in the right order if frustration and disappointment are to be avoided! The key to success is the initial elimination of established perennial weeds by means of a non-persistent systemic herbicide such as glyphosate.

Most people are anxious to control weeds because they are regarded as unsightly. However, it is often not appreciated that a strong growth of weeds has a very adverse effect on the growth of garden plants; managing without weeds may well give a bonus in improved growth and quality of trees, shrubs and herbaceous plants, as well as the time to enjoy them.

Good Gardening!

INDEX